How to Hangover

An illustrated guide

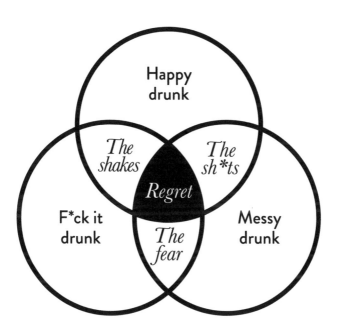

Happy drunk

The shakes

The sh*ts

Regret

F*ck it drunk

The fear

Messy drunk

Stephen Wildish

Cheers!

1 H_2O Water					

Period

Beers **Wines**

☐ Alcoholic
■ Non-alcoholic
☐ Hot drinks

		The hard s*

STRENGTH

3 La Lager	**4** Pr Prosecco			
9 Ci Cider	**10** Ch Champagne			
15 Al Ale	**16** Wi White wine	**17** Sh Sherry	**18** Vm Vermouth	**19** Sk Saki
26 Bi Bitter	**27** Ro Rosé	**28** Br Brandy	**29** Du Drambui	**30** Tq Tequilla
37 Po Porter	**38** Rd Red wine	**39** Cg Cognac	**40** Am Amaretto	**41** Ou Ouzo
48 Gu Stout	**49** Pt Port	**50** Ar Armagnac	**51** Jgm Herb liqueur	**52** Ab Absinthe

There are three main categories of drinks: alcoholic, non-alcoholic and hot drinks. The higher up on the table the lighter the drink. The columns of the table show subcategories of drinks (beer, wine, etc.) from 'light' to 'dark'. This grading encompasses strength of drink and colouring.

able of drinks

	Bitters	Milks	Fruits	Soda
	5 Bs Bitters	**6 Mi** Milk	**7 Aj** Apple juice	**8 So** Soda
	11 Su Sours	**12 Bm** Banana milk	**13 Cr** Cranberry juice	**14 Le** Lemonade

R ite rum	**21 G** Gin	**22 Tn** Tonic	**23 Sm** Strawberry milk	**24 Gj** Grape juice	**25 Cy** Cherryade
Sr ced rum	**32 Vk** Vodka	**33 Ap** Apéritif	**34 Cm** Chocolate milk	**35 Oj** Orange juice	**36 Or** Orangeade
Dr rk rum	**43 Sa** Sambuca	**44 Ck** Cocktails	**45 By** Baileys	**46 Tj** Tomato juice	**47 Gi** Ginger beer
W /hisky	**54 Ws** White spirit	**55 Li** Limoncello	**56 Ad** Advocaat	**57 Fl** Schnapps	**58 Co** Cola

59 S Soup	**60 C** Coffee	**61 T** Tea	**62 Ft** Fruit tea	**63 Hc** Hot choc

→

SWEETNESS

Contents

Introduction

Introduction

If you drink too much alcohol, a hangover is as inevitable
as night following day. In this book we will discover
how to cope with a two-dayer, a lucky escape and with
something called 'the fear'.

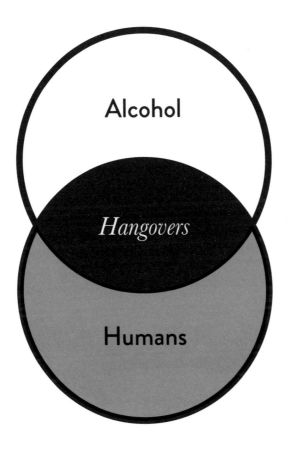

What is a hangover?

In simple terms, a hangover is what happens when you drink too much alcohol. It's the after-effects of having too much fun. A hangover is pain. Physical, mental and social pain. It is going out for a quiet pint and waking up with your entire life in ruins.

A hangover can take many forms, from a simple headache to a full body 'fuckover'. Typical symptoms include tiredness, weakness, headache, sickness, the shits, sensitivity to light, crippling anxiety and sweating like a glass-blower's arse.

One of the most curious effects of a hangover is that it causes the sufferer to mumble over and over that they will 'never drink again'. When in fact they and everyone around them knows they fully intend to 'get back on it' mere hours or days later. Sometimes a hangover can be so severe that the sufferer can be sworn off alcohol for a week or two.

A hangover is unlike any illness as it mixes all the fun of a serious affliction with the anxiety and depression of a mental-health incident. Best of all? It's all entirely self-inflicted: you did this to yourself, you fucking genius!

Waking up not knowing if you're dead
or if you need to move country out of shame

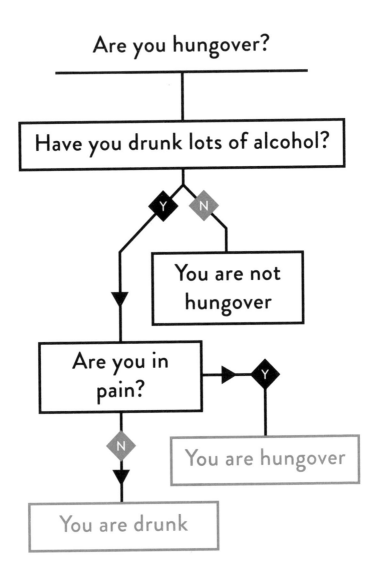

Are you hungover?

Have you drunk lots of alcohol?

Y N

You are not hungover

Are you in pain? Y

You are hungover

N

You are drunk

Calling in 'sick'

You've gone out on a 'school night' and ended up going 'out out'. It was supposed to be a quiet after-work drink in a nice pub but it ended in the only sweatbox in town serving drinks at 3am. The drink made you forget that it's not Friday and you do indeed have work in the morning.

When you wake up with a real stinker of a hangover, what can you do? Do you call in sick and claim that you have the tummy bug going around? Do you force yourself into work and have the shittest day on record pretending to be normal and trying not to be sick in a bin? Lying is never a good idea, especially if your work mates were with you for the first half of the night. They will know what went on and if the lie comes out you could end up in a worse situation than if you'd come clean. It's time to strap your big-boy trousers on and make that awkward call.

Christmas Eve drinks were a bad idea

Which drinks cause hangovers?

Rather than shots or red wine, most experts in the field argue that beer (and in particular stout and the darker, more flavoursome beers) are the very worst drinks on the bar for handing out hangovers. Not because of their content but because of their drinkability. You can down a pint but good luck downing a pint of wine (this is not a challenge). A modern IPA is touted as a superior drink for its unfiltered flavours, but guess what? When a drink is filtered it's filtering out all manner of chemicals as well. Chemicals that might just cause you an epic headache in the morning, giving you a 'head like John the Baptist'.

Are shots ever a good idea?

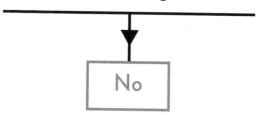

On the other hand, red wine and strong spirits do have a well-deserved reputation as hangover makers. For instance, a red wine hangover is a very special breed indeed. It consists of a stinging headache like no other, a sharp pain strong enough to pierce a hole in steel. All topped off with the strong visual of you with blue lips and teeth, really classy!

A hangover after numerous shots of tequila slammers, however, will be tinged with flashbacks to all the karaoke and the bit where you stood on the pool table and took down your trousers. Oh god, the shame. All of this through a cloud of pain and the faint taste of whatever tequila tastes of. Worms? Is it worms? I think worms are involved somewhere.

Length of a hangover

The length of a hangover is determined by two things: your age, and how much of a twat you were the night before.

As you get older, your ability to recover from hangovers decreases. In your twenties, hangovers are a mere blip in your day; in your thirties, they turn into an ordeal that requires medical help. In your forties, you may discover the delight of a two-day or even three-day hangover. What a joy!

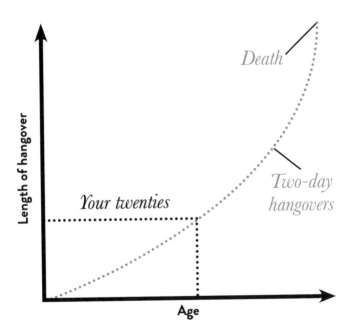

Will this be a bad hangover?

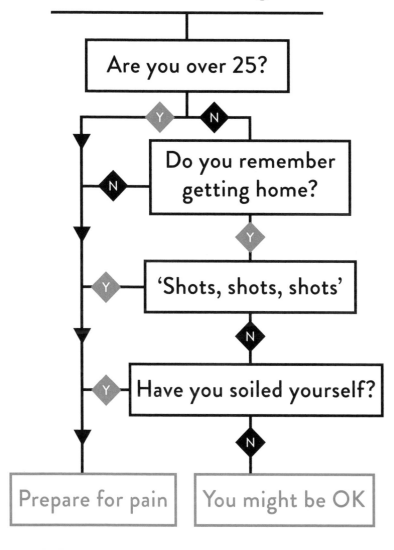

Chemistry of a hangover

Nerd alert! There will be some big words in the next paragraph. If you're just here to treat your headache so you can get back on 'the sesh' with a 'bag o' cans' then please skip to the bottom of the page.

What happens to alcohol (or ethanol) when it gets in your bloodstream? The ethanol finds its way to your liver and is converted to acetaldehyde by the dehydrogenase enzyme (I hope you're taking notes). The acetaldehyde is then further broken down to acetate. Acetate can be broken down into carbon dioxide and water and then expelled from the body (through pissing and breathing). Your liver can break down ethanol at the rate of one unit every hour.

The compound acetaldehyde, if not broken down, has some nasty toxic effects that can cause a fair few of your hangover symptoms.

Also found in your beverage are other compounds like methanol, which breaks down into formaldehyde (yes, the stuff they embalm dead bodies and sheep in art galleries with).
This isn't good news for a hangover.

Lastly, alcohol can affect the levels of a group of proteins called cytokines in your body. What are those, you ask? Just know that you probably don't want your levels disrupted.

In summary, alcohol fucks you up.
Here endeth the chemistry lesson.

Concocting the perfect hangover

History of hangovers

The first recorded hangover was described by Pliny the Elder in around AD 77. Pliny was a devoted drinker and loved writing about all things boozy. Pliny describes drunk people as pallid with drooping eyelids, and having 'dreams of monstrous lustfulness and forbidden delights'. Projecting much, Pliny?

Pliny recorded a great number of hangover cures. It's not clear how badly he was hanging out the back of his toga when he wrote this particular one but it calls for the sufferer to wear a necklace of parsley, followed by swallowing two raw owl's eggs in wine, or deep-fried decapitated canary dusted with salt and pepper. Rank, and of course entirely useless.

Another of Pliny's 'cures' consisted of garlic, oil and bread. That is clearly the recipe for a delicious garlic bread. Some of Pliny's cures have evolved into the modern-day cures we see later on (prairie oysters), some have been refined and put on the menu at Pizza Express (garlic bread) and some, luckily, have been consigned to history (fried headless canaries).

In his favour, Pliny did suggest a useful tip for preventing hangovers: lining the stomach with food before drinking. To his detriment his preferred meal for this was roast sheep's intestines.

Pliny the Pisshead

Phrases for hangovers

There's something about the pain of a hangover that spurs creative poetry in the sufferer. The puerility of the phrase will depend on the level of the hangover; the more pain, the more filth. Popular phrases fall into three categories:

Arse and shit

I feel like {
I've licked a badger's arse

dog shit that's been stepped in twice

a boiled turd
}

The head metaphors

I have a head {
full of wasps

like a burst mattress

like a bag of chisels
}

The mad ones

I'm {
on my beeriod

suffering from wine flu

as sick as a small hospital
}

How the world describes its hangovers

Origin	Phrase	Meaning
Danish	Tømmermænd	A builder with a hammer
French	Mal aux cheveux	My hair hurts
French	J'ai la gueule de bois	My gob is made from wood
German	Einen Kater haben	The wailing of cats
Icelandic	Thynnka	I'm...thin...
Irish	Having the brown bottle flu	I drank too much stout
Italian	Ho i postumi della sbornia	The after-death of drunkenness
Japanese	Futsuka-yoi shiteru!	Two days drunk!

Samuel Pepys

Famous diary scribbler and cheese burier Samuel Pepys
noted in his diary on New Year's Day 1661 that his hangover
remedy breakfast served up to his guests consists of:
'a barrel of oysters, a plate of cow's tongues, a plate of
anchovies, wine of all sorts and Northdown ale'. You
probably have most of that in the fridge, right? If not,
pop down Londis, they will probably have it in.

Elsewhere in his diaries he recommends a hangover
cure with less of a Henry VIII vibe. He suggests drinking
'chocolate from a chocolate house'. The real news here is
that there used to be chocolate houses in the 1600s.

Gout

'Gout? What are you talking about?' you may ask. Gout isn't just some Victorian-style disease that olden-days people contracted like consumption or the pox. Gout is very much real and a very painful problem if you're a big drinker.

Gout can be brought on by drinking too much alcohol and eating rich foods (gorging on mead and pheasant like a medieval king). The condition starts with your kidneys deciding that you're a prick for eating and drinking too much. Instead of breaking down and processing uric acid they send it back around your bloodstream. When uric acid finds a lovely cold joint (typically your big toe), it forms giant, sharp crystals. Piss crystals are then in your blood, causing you a whole world of pain.

Gout isn't typical of a hangover but can be brought on by a night on the grog and may last for days or weeks.

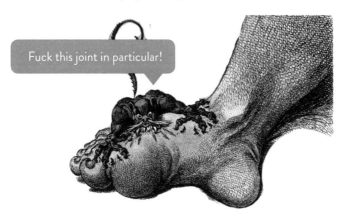

Are you going to die?

Are you really hungover?

You will die one day,
but probably not today

Feel like you're dying?

Although it may feel like it, you can't die from a hangover. Hangovers are your body's way of dealing with all the toxins you stuck in it for some reason last night. They are the punishment for having all that fun. As Dolly Parton once said, 'If you want the rainbow, you gotta put up with the rain.' In the case of a bad hangover, the raindrops in this metaphor are hailstones as big as golf balls.

You may hear people with a stinking hangover claim they have alcohol poisoning. Whilst amusing to say, it's very rarely true. A good rule of thumb is that if you can talk, you don't have alcohol poisoning.

"IN VINO VERITAS"

"IN WINE THERE IS TRUTH"

Pliny the Elder

Hangover types

Hangover types

You awaken, your eyes barely open; they're like piss holes in the snow. Your head is pounding and there is the aroma of vomit in the air. Wait, is that kebab on the wall?!

Congratulations, you have a raging hangover. But which type? There are many different varieties in this wonderful dark rainbow of pain, so let's discover some well-known and some less well-known types of hangover.

Identifying what hangover you have

If you are waking up with (or in some cases without) a hangover, the first thing to work out is exactly what hangover you are experiencing. Equipped with this knowledge, you can set about curing yourself in the best possible way. If you are violently vomiting down a toilet then I suggest you put the book down and concentrate on the job at hand – it's bloody obvious which hangover you have: the exorcist.

There are many symptoms that overlap and are present in most hangovers. A headache, aches, pains and general fatigue are a given.

There are other types of hangover not documented here because they are too rare or specific to a single symptom or alcoholic drink – for example a red wine hangover or an absinthe meltdown. You're just going to have to find a best match for these.

Needing a crane to move alcohol equates to a monumental hangover

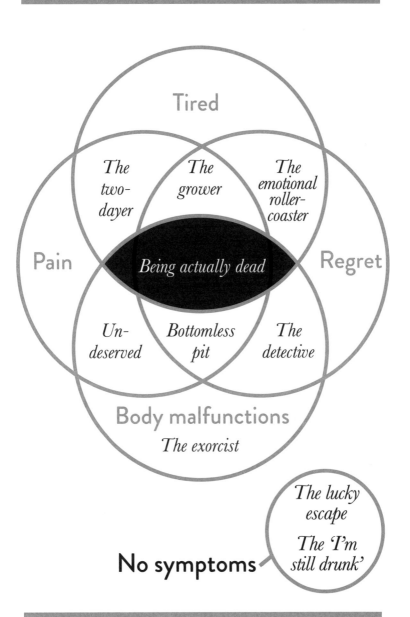

The lucky escape

You've drunk enough to drop a decent-sized elephant, you had no regard for your own safety and you treated your liver like it had pissed on your kids. But here you are, waking up without a hangover at all. Nothing. Nada.

You remember everything; you remember the taxi home and falling in the bush outside your house. So what gives? How have you escaped the hangover? There are two theories:

You are still pissed
You are currently being numbed by the sheer volume of alcohol in your system. Your hangover is on pre-order for later this afternoon; it's coming *(see page 53)*. Best get some sleep in preparation.

You managed to sleep enough
For some reason or another, your body managed to get enough sleep last night so the tired effects of a hangover are not hitting you first. As you are well rested, your body is also processing the alcohol in your system better than if you were knackered. Lucky you!

Take it easy though – don't go roller blading or rock climbing just yet, you could just be delusional and in fact be suffering from the first option. You are, in fact, still pissed.

**Experiencing a lucky escape hangover
and feeling invincible**

This calls for a celebration!
See page 142 for a recipe for a bloody mary.

The 'I'm still drunk'

The 'I'm still drunk' hangover feels like you're still drunk, because guess what? You're still drunk, you moron. The tell-tale signs of an 'I'm still drunk' hangover are:

Finding things funny

Finding the whole situation funny, still laughing about the awful jokes from last night and showing little to no remorse about your awful actions. Do you remember talking to that guy? Do you? It was bad: you slurred and repeated yourself – but you don't seem to care, do you?

No signs of a hangover

Waking up thinking you've escaped a hangover: lucky you! You're pain-free, with no sickness or any real symptoms at all. Oh, don't you worry, the hangover will catch you. It's only a matter of time before it rains down on you. Hard.

Up to larks

With an 'I'm still drunk' hangover you can miraculously still get up to japes and continue the antics on from the night before. Much to the utter annoyance of those around you who are suffering with the more standard hangovers. However, it's worth bearing in mind the previous point about the hangover tracking you down; it will and if you're very unlucky it could be mid skulduggery.

Generally speaking, it takes about six hours from when you finish drinking for the 'drunk' effects of alcohol to wear off. If you wake up with an 'I'm still drunk' hangover, then presumably you drank enough to sedate a Shire horse or alternatively you have not been asleep yet.

There are plenty of myths about how to get alcohol through your body quicker but it's all to do with your liver function and how much punishment you've put it through over the years. So what can you do?

Get some sleep

You're just playing the waiting game until the effects wear off so try to get some more sleep if you can.

Continue drinking

Maintain an even keel, the fine balance between tipsy and plastered. Obviously don't do this if you need to be at work or operate heavy machinery ... or operate heavy machinery at work.

If you feel competent enough to crack a couple of eggs, turn to page 118 for the scrambled egg recipe.

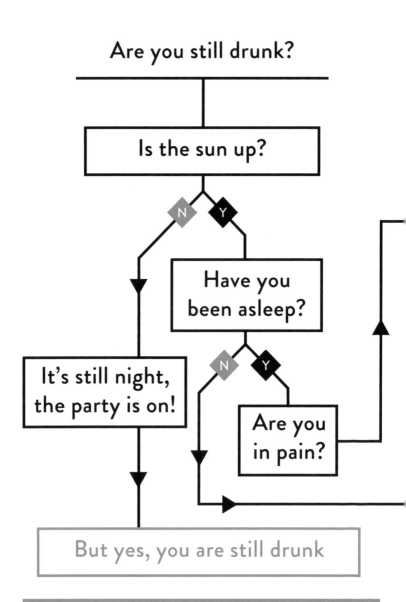

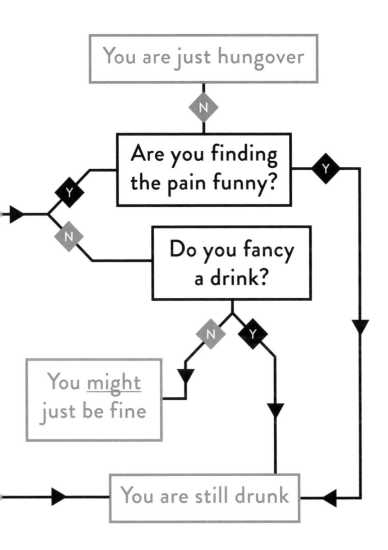

You are just hungover

N

Are you finding the pain funny?

Y

Y

N

Do you fancy a drink?

N

Y

You <u>might</u> just be fine

You are still drunk

The bottomless pit

The bottomless pit hangover manifests itself as a search for the perfect food item that will remove all the negative feelings you are currently experiencing. It's a fruitless search as no food on earth will make up for the amount of cheap alcohol you drank last night.

The bottomless pit hangover tends to appear in the mornings after for day drinkers or people who have skipped meals during the drinking session the previous night. Your low blood sugar would be making you hungry anyway but as this has been magnified by the alcohol intake you've poured down your neck, you wake up absolutely ravenous.

"EATING IS CHEATING"

Day drinkers

So what is going on – why do you not get full on a bottomless pit hangover? Why is your body doing this to you?

You're probably craving food that is hot, brown, high in fat and salty. Although this could also describe a fresh dog shit, please have some awareness of what you are eating.

In this hungover state your body is seriously craving those really un-complex carbs to restore its levels of glycogen. Food high in fat, salt and sugar begin to look dreamier than ever. Whilst you are frantically stuffing pizza and doughnuts in your dribbling face, the messages from your gut to your brain telling it that it has had 'enough now, stop ... for the love of god, stop' are being delayed as the alcohol in your system is suppressing a hormone called leptin. This wonderful hormone tells your brain when you are full. Without it you're a hungry hippo and your kitchen is the marble playground.

Eat enough shit and you're going to start feeling even more shit; go too far and your body might even stage a coup and make you puke it all up.

Well then, at least you can start again – get yourself back to the beige buffet, more nuggets please.

I know it will be tempting to stuff your face with a huge full English (see page 123) but maybe try to eat something more nutritious for once in your life.

A typical day with a bottomless pit hangover

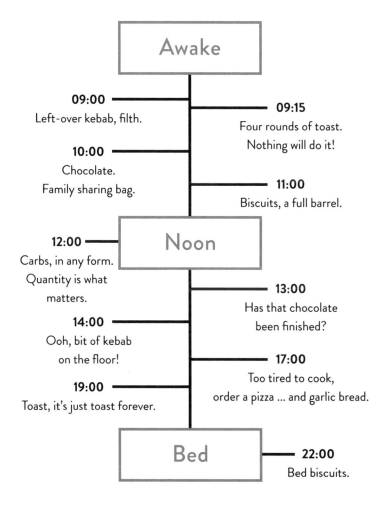

Awake

09:00
Left-over kebab, filth.

09:15
Four rounds of toast.
Nothing will do it!

10:00
Chocolate.
Family sharing bag.

11:00
Biscuits, a full barrel.

Noon

12:00
Carbs, in any form.
Quantity is what
matters.

13:00
Has that chocolate
been finished?

14:00
Ooh, bit of kebab
on the floor!

17:00
Too tired to cook,
order a pizza ... and garlic bread.

19:00
Toast, it's just toast forever.

Bed

22:00
Bed biscuits.

A two-dayer

You awaken the day after the day after and you're still hungover. 'What the fuck is going on?' you may ask, and you would be entirely justified in doing so. This hardly seems fair; two days of hangover is enough to make you swear off drinking for a good while. So why have you been cursed with such a burden? The answer may lie in your recovery, your age or just how legendary the original night out was.

What if it's a three-dayer?

A 'two-dayer' becomes a reality in your life after you turn 30. The first one will come as a bit of a shock, but after they have turned up once in your life they will turn up again, like a bad penny. A stinking bad penny, laced with poison, remorse and pain.

A two-day hangover is even more likely if you've dealt with the first day poorly. If you get enough sleep and drink enough water you might be OK but if you believed some bullshit hangover cures that include alcohol then you are basically signing up for day two of the same shit.

Another reason for a two-day hangover could be a secondary infection or symptom – for example, you spent the day chucking up. Mix this with some tiredness and your body not working at 100 per cent and voila! You just gave yourself the shits. A whole new world of shit that you have to deal with. Literally.

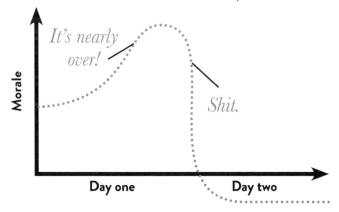

See 'not being old' as an ideal cure for a two-dayer hangover.

The undeserved

You drank a glass of water before going to bed, you remember everything, you behaved yourself and yet you've just woken up and your head is hanging out of your arse. You have an undeserved hangover.

But why? Why has your body chosen to do this to you? You were good. You didn't have any of the fun associated with a hangover but all of the pain. This is totally unfair.

One explanation is that you drank some shitty wine full of sulphites, tannins and histamine that have clogged up your nerves and pipes (yes, that is the medical term). To avoid an undeserved hangover maybe don't purchase the cheapest bottle of red from the petrol station? Think of it as self-care.

	What are they for?	How do they affect you?	How do they make you feel?
Sulphites	Preserving things	If you have a sulphite sensitivity, badly	Like shit
Tannins	Found in grape skins	Tannins cause you to release too much serotonin	Too much serotonin leads to migraines. Poor you
Histamine	Found in cheap wine	Histamine dilates blood vessels	Dilated blood vessels; throbbing headache

Do you deserve this hangover?

Did you drink like an arsehole?

Y N

This is simply unfair

You deserve everything

Dilute sulphites, tannins and histamine by drinking plenty of water – see page 102.

Illness

You could of course just be legitimately ill; many of the symptoms of a hangover are also that of illness but just not self-inflicted, e.g. a headache, aches and pains and general malaise. This might not explain why you shit yourself in a taxi on the way home though – that's not illness, mate, there's no excuse for that.

You didn't sleep well

Like the illness above, being overly tired is a large part of what a hangover feels like, so if you can get some more sleep you will more than likely awaken in a few hours feeling refreshed. If for some reason you can't, then your day is about to suck really hard.

The grower

The grower hangover is an amalgamation of the 'I'm still drunk' hangover and the 'lucky escape' hangover. You wake up and think you've had a lucky escape; you're on top of the world. What has happened is that you have woken up still a little bit pissed, which has acted as an anaesthetic. As this wears off, the true horror of your hangover starts to reveal itself. By midday you've got the sweats, a headache from hell and the world has fallen out of your arse, like a rusty tap. The good thing about a grower hangover is that because it hits you later in the day you only have a few hours to wait it out until you can go to bed that evening.

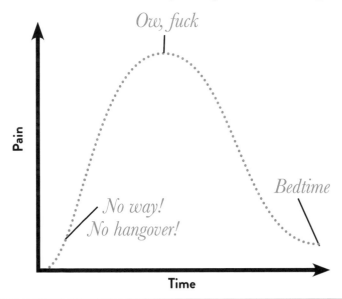

Try to consume as many nutrients as you can before the hangover hits – see page 119 to learn why bananas are crucial.

The emotional roller-coaster

You're sitting up in bed, the physical effects of the hangover
are mild but for some reason you can't stop crying.

Oh god! It's coming back to you, when you said that thing to the
barman. You talked a lot of shit last night. Oh no, remember when you
tried to slut drop and your trousers split? You did manage to get home
without stealing a traffic cone for your collection, though: go you!

Alcohol is a depressant, not – as some think – a stimulant. It depresses
every one of your senses in turn (it depresses your common sense first).
Alcohol depresses your nervous system and can affect the production
of dopamine (the happy hormone). So you wake up depleted of 'happy'.
Mix that up with some malaise, tiredness and a general level of regret
and you have the perfect cocktail for a decent crying session.

There's nothing for it but to stick on a rom-com and wait this one out,
as you try to get those serotonin and dopamine levels back up.

Oh, the consequences of my actions have arrived

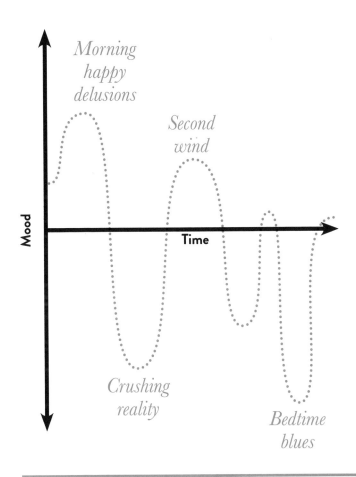

See page 107 to learn about crying as a cure for this
hangover. Put a Disney Movie on, it's time to regress.

The exorcist

You've spent the night crouched over the toilet projectile vomiting green bile. There is nothing you can do to stop it. The exorcist hangover has more in store for you than just near-constant vomiting of horrific green bile, there is also a six-hour period of lying in bed too sick to sleep and too tired to move to look forward to. It really is one of the worst hangovers to have. You may recover, but you may have to clean the bathroom with a hazmat suit. We shall rebuild.

The only saving grace of an exorcist hangover is that you are so occupied with the physical needs of the hangover (running to the toilet without slipping on sick) that there is no time to reflect upon your awful behaviour last night, no time to check your messages and socials to see the karaoke video, yes you did sing and yes it was bad. Oh god, was it bad.

ARRRRGGGHHHHHHHHHH

An exorcist hangover can be brought on by dodgy late-night vittles purchased in a fast-food establishment where the 'chefs' have no obvious place to clean their hands or, as we strongly suspect, your stomach is not up to the amount of tequilas you slammed or the snakebites you chugged.

Set up camp in the bathroom and try to stay hydrated as best you can. Get a Berocca and take small but frequent sips of water to start replenishing the nutrients lost by the near-constant regurgitations. It's going to be a long day ... You can feel another wave coming. 'Fuck that kebab van, fuck him and his rubbery burger.'

Replace lost nutrients as quickly as you can – see page 134 for more information on isotonic sports drinks.

The detective

As your eyelids peel back over your crusty eyeballs, you realise you're in pain. But you have no idea why. 'Why does everything hurt?' It takes a moment for you to remember your name, to remember where you are. 'Did I go out last night?', 'What is happening?'

As myriad questions fill your brain, some of the basic answers come back to you. Yes, you went out, just for a quiet one. Yes, you're at home. So far so good. So what happened between the hours of 9pm and now?

You are now taking on the role of the mystery detective. You begin to scour your phone for clues; all your photos are investigated for any tell-tale signs. Is that a clock in the background of that photo? That means you were at the usual bar at 10pm. Ooh, a card transaction at 1am for a round of flaming sambuccas. That's not good.

You're now the Pissed-up-Poirot, assembling your night out on a table in front of you. It's time to get some suspects involved, call the gang, start to piece things together and prepare your apologies for the inevitable social clean-up.

So what is happening to cause a memory-mystery hangover? If you manage to drink enough alcohol on a night out, your brain just gives up recording short-term memories, leading to holes in your recollection of what happened the previous night. It's not something you want to be doing a lot of.

> Call your trusted mate to help you piece together
> the evening and get your apologies ready.

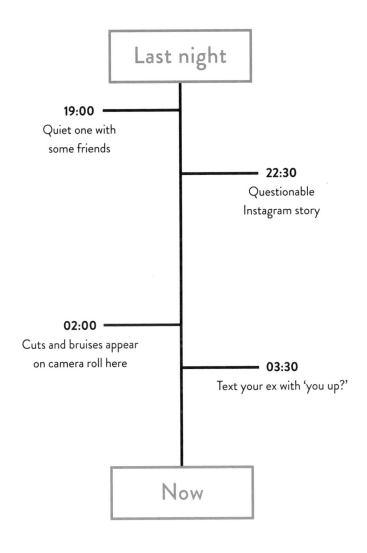

Last night

19:00
Quiet one with
some friends

22:30
Questionable
Instagram story

02:00
Cuts and bruises appear
on camera roll here

03:30
Text your ex with 'you up?'

Now

"HANGOVERS ARE TEMPORARY MEMORIES ARE PERMANENT"

The fable

"THE LAST THING I REMEMBER WAS DRINKING FROM A SHOE"

Reality

The fear, the shits and the shakes

The fear, the shits and the shakes

Yes, you are reading a book with a chapter about having the shits. What a brilliant road your life has led you to. At least you are not having to write it. The fear, the shits and the shakes are the three worst hangover symptoms there are, so bad in fact that they deserve their own chapter.

They affect you mentally, physically and socially (especially if your shits have been sprayed around the local pub). God help you if you have all three at once!

The fear

The fear, Sunday scaries or hangxiety is the wave of overwhelming, mind-numbing anxiety and regret that can overtake the physical symptoms of a hangover. Shuddering moments of crystal clarity of how you acted like a complete twat last night. The same moments playing over in your head ad infinitum.

The fear's paralysing cringe effect on your body could be down to a few factors:

Running on empty
Your body is tired and low on endorphins (you used all of them up last night singing in the kebab shop). Having little in the way of sleep will certainly affect your mood and cause your symptoms to be worse.

Folic acid
Low folic acid levels can also affect your mood – and what causes low folic acid levels? Quelle surprise, it's alcohol.

Memory loss
Having black holes in your memory of the previous evening can lead you to fill in the gaps with terrible versions of what actually happened.

Fuck around and find out
You can't blame all this regret and anxiety on your folic acid levels though. As you are well aware, the primary cause of the fear is you fucking around last night and right now you are in the 'finding out' portion of that popular phrase.

How to cure the fear

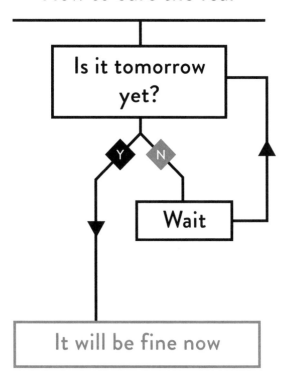

Texting for help

First things first, check your social media for any immediate damage limitation needed. Then it's time to start texting all of your mates (the ones you trust) with questions fishing for reassurance. 'Did we go out last night?', 'Was I OK?', 'Did I try to bed the bouncer again?'

A good friend will help you out and assure you that everything was OK even if that is far from the truth. Providing much-needed comfort and easing of the fear ... Even better friends will lay it all out for you in all its cringey glory. No punches pulled. You were a twat, they know it and they are about to show you the horrific video evidence.

Keep watching, you're about to fall over again!

The shits

You could be one of the lucky ones and find that a restorative morning-after poo is a vital first step on the road to recovery, but for many a hangover can spell a case of the chronic beer-shits But why? Why you and why now?!

Alcohol affects every organ in your body, including your intestines (yeah, you didn't think of that when you were ordering a Bailey's and Aftershock shot last night, did you?). Alcohol stops your gut's abilities to absorb water and nutrients, which leads to bloating. Add into this mix the grease-fest of food you scoffed down last night as if it was your last meal on earth after the crate of acidic beer and cheap wine. Your intestines are now packed full of watery, semi-digested food and booze with only one way out...

Congratulations, you have the shits!

It's explosive, and it won't stop. You can spend a good 40 minutes shitting your brains out only to go lie down and have to run back to the loo to cough out some more bile from your bottom.

But it's not all bad news. Just kidding. It's all bad news. Managing a case of after-grog-bog whilst also managing your other hangover symptoms is one of life's finest challenges. Your body will be feeling weak anyway from the low blood sugar and the incessant diarrhoea will be making you sweat and feel even weaker.

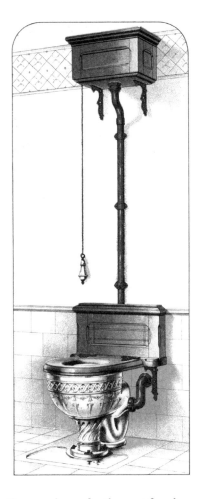

Your new home for the next four hours

Because there is no infection in the bowels, the shits caused by a hangover should pass fairly quickly, usually dealt with in three or four hours. It's a waiting game. You, waiting on the toilet, for this to be over.

First aid
Keep drinking water. If you have it, sparkling water will help settle your tummy; we don't know how, the secret is in the bubbles. Avoid any dairy or overly fatty foods, as these just place strain on your already tired intestines. You can eat bananas and toast as these foods help settle everything down. If even they are too much for you, some plain, salty crackers will do the job.

Secondary infection
If you are amazingly unlucky you could develop a reaction to a certain type of alcohol you might be sensitive to, or, worse, you could develop food poisoning. If you picked up a suspiciously pink chicken burger from a dodgy van in a layby served by a chap who gave you extra onions with a cheeky wink, what did you think would happen?

If your shits are more violent, generally getting worse and not better and if the whole ordeal has lasted more than two days it is time to seek professional help. A funeral director.

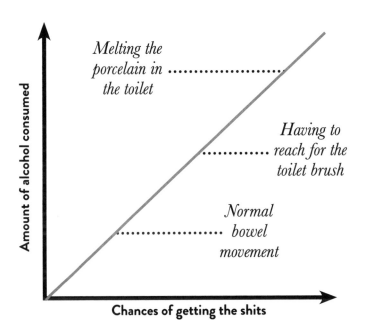

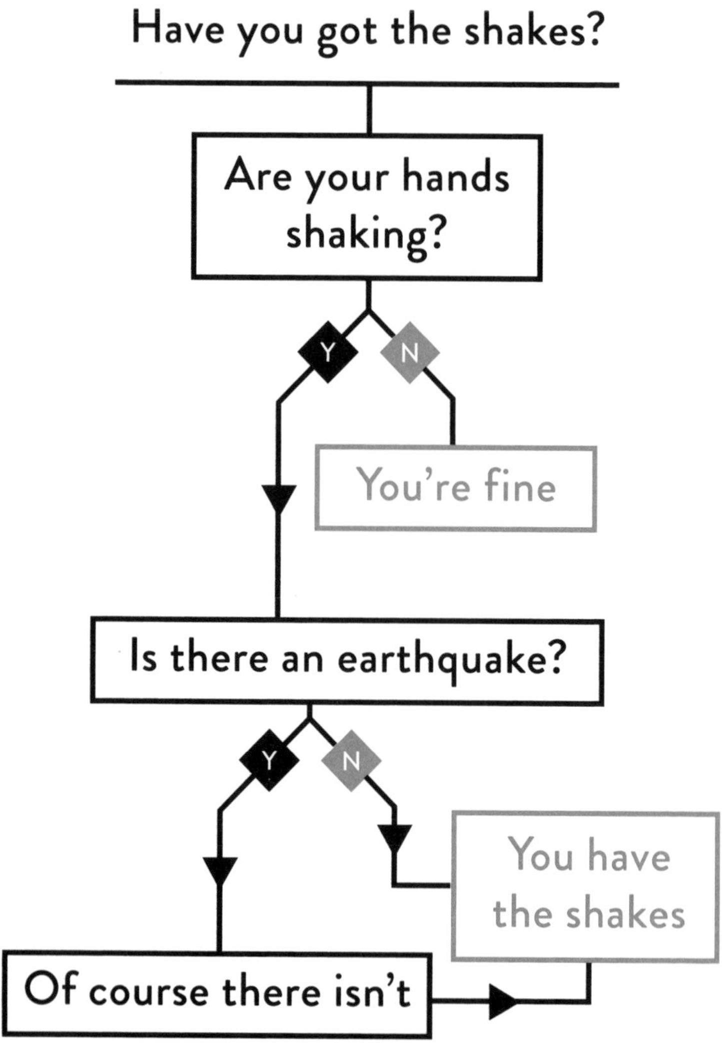

Have you got the shakes?

Are your hands shaking?

Y — N

You're fine

Is there an earthquake?

Y — N

You have the shakes

Of course there isn't

The shakes

The shakes are the least-welcome guest at the very worst and most extreme hangover parties – though it might take you a little while to register what is going on when you have them.

Hangover shakes manifest themselves as a trembling feeling all over combined with hot and cold sweats. The tell-tale hand shake is the most obvious symptom. Trying to write your name on the police officer's bail paperwork with the shakes is a dead giveaway that you are having one hell of a hangover.

Cause of the shakes

What is causing your feeble little trembles? There are a few ways you can have the shakes. The alcohol could be slowing down your nervous system's normally lightning-quick speeds and misfiring signals all over the place, resulting in tremors and lack of balance (i.e. your nerves are plastered).

Alternatively, you could be suffering from a mild version of alcohol withdrawal. The amount of booze you drank has affected your nervous system and triggered an over-reactive response and it wants to have more alcohol to feel 'normal' again. Your body is now craving alcohol. If you do give in and have a hair-of-the-dog cure you could have a miraculous, albeit short-lived, resurrection. A small amount of alcohol will cure the shakes and sweats almost instantly. But all you've really done is kicked the problem down the road. As soon as that drink wears off, the shakes will be back with you.

Avoiding the shakes

The most obvious option for avoiding the shakes is not drinking enough alcohol to floor a full rugby league team in the first place. But clearly you're not going to do that.

If you have any forethought at all make sure you eat well before drinking and drink water throughout the evening session or before you go to bed. Try to go to bed at a decent time to allow your body to sleep it off.

Treating the shakes

Drinking water and getting a good breakfast will certainly speed up your body's response to the alcohol and will help you process the alcohol left in your system quicker. Plain porridge and toast with fruit will boost your sugar levels and give you some helpful easy-access carb energy.

If you are a hardened long-term drinker these shakes can start to become more common. You're now into the 'damaging your body irreparably' category of drinking. If your symptoms are not easing after a day then it could be that you have something more serious going on, so stop googling it and reading about it in a silly book – make an appointment with a doctor to get yourself checked out.

YOU CALL IT A "HANGOVER"

I LIKE TO CALL IT CALL IT "FUN TAX"

The clean-up

The clean-up

Apart from the irreparable damage you've caused your kidney and liver in the past 24 hours there is the small matter of the absolute bomb-site to clear up! There are many, many fluids everywhere. Some human, some chemical, some ... animal? 'God, is that a dead chicken in the corner?', 'Anyone know how to get a pentagram out of a shag pile?'

Upon opening your phone there are hundreds of unwanted notifications and messages that need desperate attention, so a social cleanse is also completely necessary.

Restoring the house/community centre/squat to good order after the party/rave/satanic ritual has finished can cleanse the mind and make you feel physically better. Grab a mop and bucket, it's time to face that pile of vomit left by Uncle John.

Realising you sent the mother-in-law a cheeky text
and a questionable nude that was meant for your wife

Cleaning up vomit

If you've not been lucky enough to make it to the loo in the night a pile of vomit can often be found by the bed, in the bed or up the stairs. Discovering a 'technicolour yawn' by stepping in it is quite the experience, one not to be repeated often.

Aside from the contents of your stomach, vomit is full of lots of lovely acids and chemicals that are perfect for leaving a stain and a smell. Once you get rid of the main bulk of the vomit you're going to need to get some proper industrial chemicals down to neutralise this health hazard.

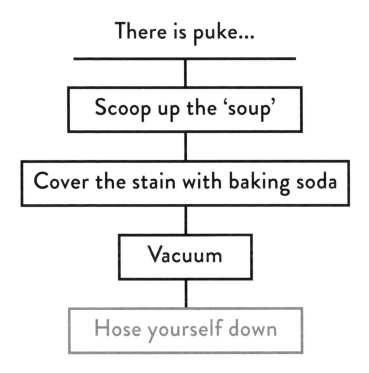

There is puke...

Scoop up the 'soup'

Cover the stain with baking soda

Vacuum

Hose yourself down

Cleaning up piss

Piss can find its way into very unusual places after a night on the grog. It's not uncommon for a weary drinker to stumble from their bed and mistake a wardrobe, radiator or cat's bed for the toilet and continue to fill it to the brim with hot beery piss. Worse still is if they don't manage to get up and just piss the bed.

So how do you get piss out of a wardrobe? Fuck knows. A sponge is a good start. Probably. Let's look at a much more common scenario – a bed full of piss.

Clean the sheets

This is the easy part: get the sheets off the bed, put them in the washing machine. If you have a bedfellow that doesn't realise you've pissed the bed, now is the right time to break the news to them.

Cleaning the mattress

Piss will dry fairly quickly, leaving a pungent aroma, so it's good to get cracking whilst it's still wet. Get a solution of water and white wine vinegar, sponge down the mattress and dry off with a towel. Put the towel in the washing machine immediately, in case you forget and use it after the shower.

If you don't want your mattress to smell like a chip shop for months after, you can use a mixture of baking soda, soap and bleach to sponge down the offending stain. Baking soda is a natural deodoriser and should remove most of the smell. But there will always be the lingering hum of piss if you get too close.

Dealing with your bedfellow
After all the emergency piss cleaning has ceased it's time to deal
with the bedfellow who is, rightly, outraged by your actions. The
clean-up you've already performed is a good start so make sure you
do it to the best of your current hungover abilities.

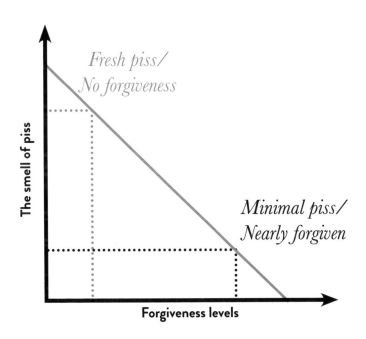

Cleaning up shit

Piles of shit can sometimes be found after a night's drinking, be it in your trousers, next to the toilet or smears up the walls. You need to clean up shit sooner rather than later. The longer you leave it the harder it will be (both figuratively and metaphorically).

Shit in clothing

Try to get any remaining solids to 'roll' out into the toilet bowl. This will cause you to heave on a good day never mind when hungover, so get ready to use the toilet to be sick into. Great, you've been sick on top of your own shit, that's an image that will haunt you for the rest of your life.

Soft furnishings

Get a big bowl of soapy water, some bleach and some sponges you don't mind never seeing again. Scrub, rinse, repeat until you've got it clean. Then rinse yourself in the shower, crouch in the corner and rock back and forth until you are clean.

Cleaning up blood

'Whose blood is this?', 'It's not my blood', 'Should we call the police?' These are all things you'll find yourself saying when you find blood after a night of drinking. If the blood has a valid reason for being there (e.g. you bumped into a table) then you can start to clean up.

When blood is exposed to air the protein in the blood causes it to clot and this heals wounds. It's this same clotting quality of blood that causes problems when it comes to getting it out of clothes and linen. The blood binds to the fabric and the longer you leave it the harder it will be to clean. If the stain is very fresh then a rinse with cold water will do the trick. Dried blood will take a bit more work:

Soak
Soak the stain in cold water to try to break it up, leaving it for 15-minute periods.

Scrub
Soapy water and a sponge are your weapons of choice; it's a fruitless effort but worth a try.

Repeat
It's going to take some patience. Rinse and repeat a few times until you have lost the will to live.

Go nuclear
If you're still scrubbing after an hour it's time to give up with the soapy water and go nuclear. Get down the shops for some bleach and enzymatic cleaner and strap on those Marigolds!

Social media clean-up

Life before social media and smart phones was a lot easier. You could go out and cause all manner of havoc and nothing will have been recorded or remembered. On the rare occasion someone did have a camera they would have had to go and get the film processed and have one solitary copy of the offending photo that they could show to one person at a time. At the very worst they could make some photocopies.

A night out now is a very different story. Social updates will be going up as and when the chaos happens. Yes, the video of you break-dancing without your trousers has already been seen by your mum and all your mum's friends and over a thousand other people. It's a bloody nightmare. It's all fuel for 'the fear'.

You wake up and check your phone: 150 notifications. Fuck! Check your story to find out what happened, delete the evidence and quick! Aside from combating your physical symptoms, you now have to cleanse your timeline from any unwanted tags in photos, delete the rambling nonsense update you thought was funny last night and send a few apology texts to loved ones.

It's also a wise move to check your Amazon and eBay accounts for any inebriated purchases made in the heat of a tequila-fuelled haze. If you're quick you can cancel the garden flamingo tiki bar.
Oh fuck, it's been shipped.

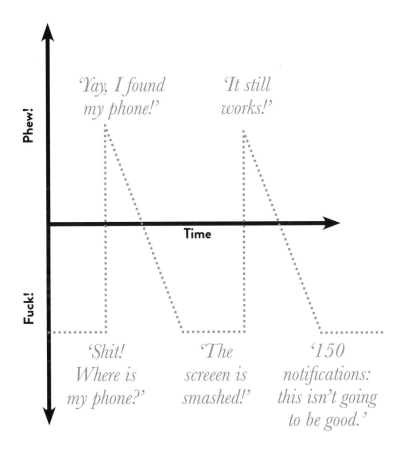

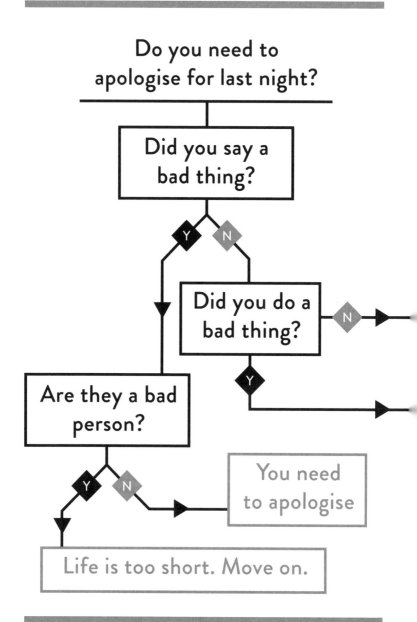

Do you need to
apologise for last night?

Did you say a
bad thing?

Y N

Did you do a
bad thing?

N

Y

Are they a bad
person?

Y N

You need
to apologise

Life is too short. Move on.

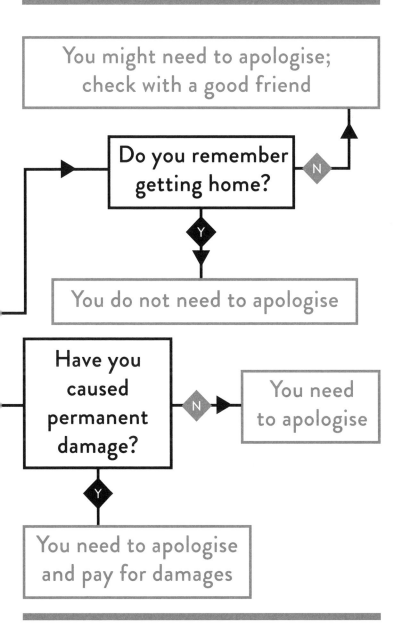

You might need to apologise; check with a good friend

Do you remember getting home?

N

Y

You do not need to apologise

Have you caused permanent damage?

N

You need to apologise

Y

You need to apologise and pay for damages

Future-proof your socials

Alcohol and social media are a particularly dangerous mix. The alcohol will be telling you how funny or knowledgeable you are, but the cold light of day will say another thing about your particularly edgy jokes and dumb insights into politics. No.

After a skin-full of drinks, your inhibitions stripped away, you're more likely to share way too many personal details online. Forgetting there is a crowd of sober people eagerly refreshing, waiting for the next stupid comment you're about to make.

To prevent this from happening, plan ahead.

Go private
Make your profiles private. You're not an influencer who needs thousands of followers, after all. Maintain a small social profile with a select group of fellow piss-head friends, thus excluding any unwanted tags and mentions.

Save as a draft
Take the questionable photo or type in your joke by all means, just save as a draft post. If it is still funny in the morning then post. The likelihood is that of course it's not and you can delete the post without it ever having to disgrace the public domain.

"DANCE LIKE NOBODY IS WATCHING"

Vodka

"READER...
EVERYBODY
WAS
WATCHING"

Cold light of day

Survival
guide

Survival guide

Surviving a hangover is all about triaging your symptoms, finding some quick wins that turn down the worst symptoms from 11 to at best a three or four on the 'oh my god' scale.

The first survival tip is to remind yourself that a hangover isn't for ever, although it might feel like it right now. This shall pass. It might take some time and a hell of a clean-up effort, but it shall pass.

Anatomy of a hangover

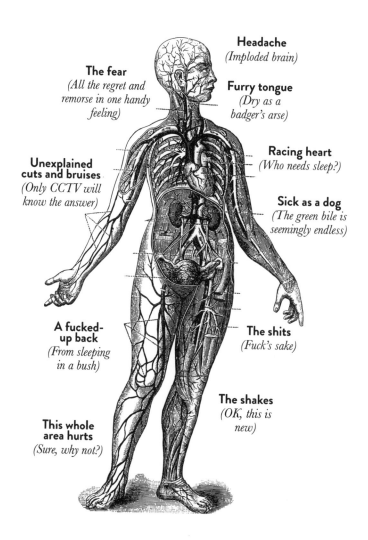

Headache
(Imploded brain)

The fear
(All the regret and remorse in one handy feeling)

Furry tongue
(Dry as a badger's arse)

Unexplained cuts and bruises
(Only CCTV will know the answer)

Racing heart
(Who needs sleep?)

Sick as a dog
(The green bile is seemingly endless)

A fucked-up back
(From sleeping in a bush)

The shits
(Fuck's sake)

The shakes
(OK, this is new)

This whole area hurts
(Sure, why not?)

Water

Alcohol is a diuretic, which means it makes you piss more. Resulting in you having less water in your body. You're turning into a raisin and you need to stop that process fast.

Dehydration causes you to feel tired, gives you a headache and makes your mouth feel like it's made from old sandals. Fortunately, dehydration is quickly reversed by drinking water. I know! How revolutionary.

In place of water, if it takes your fancy, you can drink builder's tea, green tea, soda water or flavoured waters but stay away from energy drinks and citrus juices. Although they sound like they might help, they can actually irritate the gut, prolonging the hangover symptoms. Your stomach will thank you!

Chugging your third pint of water in the morning

Recommended for: All hangovers

Exercise

You may rightly be thinking 'What the actual fuck are you talking about?' when you see the word 'exercise' suggested as a way to survive a hangover. But for a medium to mild hangover, a short, steady exercise session can stimulate your body and spring you awake. Getting your heart pumping and the blood flowing will feel great afterwards, just not before or during.

Weight training is not advised as your risk of fainting will be elevated and you will end up on one of those gym fail videos alongside someone who spews their guts up and passes out trying to deadlift a small car.

If it's all too much for you, maybe consider popping on your Gymshark twin-set and swiftly walking to the shops to get a protein bar and an energy drink so you can just pretend you went to the gym.

Absolutely not

Recommended for: Light to medium hangovers
Not recommended for: The exorcist hangover

Jogging

Imagine how smug you will feel after a crisp jog on a cold day when you've chased away a fuzzy head and got your 10,000 steps in all before 10am.

Now imagine being sick in a bush because you underestimated how hungover you were and now you have to walk two miles home with beery vomit down your activewear. Shameful.

If you are planning a jog to sort your hangover make sure it is just that, a jog. You're not going to be setting any new PBs with a hangover so hold back and let your legs take you at whatever pace they've got.

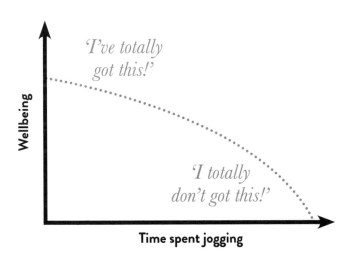

Recommended for: Light to medium hangovers
Not recommended for: The exorcist hangover

Cold-water swimming

A dunk in some ice-cold water is a fantastic way to forget about a hangover, because you will be too busy shouting, *'FUCKINGGGFUCKTHISISSHITTINGCOLD!'*

Cold water provides a massive shock to your tired system. It gives you an instant wake up and burst of energy. It can also help with a headache as your blood vessels contract from the cold, causing that throbbing feeling to dissipate. After swimming in cold water your body will get a wonderful rush of endorphins and you will begin to feel instantly better.

Even better than all these physical benefits of cold water are the bragging rights on social media. Look forward to sharing a pained selfie from an icy lake and tagging in Wim Hof #coldwatertherapy #smug.

The sea, a lake or river are all ideal for a dunk (if safe to do so). If you are nowhere near open water then you can fill a bath with cold water and sit in it for a minute or two. After your dunk, dry off and wrap up warm. You do not want to add hypothermia to your current hangover symptoms.

If you are still drunk then don't go for a swim, don't be stupid.

I can't feel my legs

Recommended for: A light to medium hangover
Not recommended for: The worst hangovers

Cry

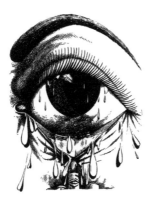

As we know, alcohol is a depressant and not a stimulant,
so the after-effects of alcohol will be a lingering depression.
Add tiredness and anxiety in there and you've got a good
recipe for tears.

Sometimes it's just best to give in and let all that emotion out.
Allow it to take over and have a good cry.
That's it, let it all out. A good ugly cry.

When you cry, you literally cry out stress hormones, thus relieving
stress and anxiety. If you cry for a good few minutes your body will start
to produce chemicals to counteract the tears, one of which is called
oxytocin. Oxytocin is sometimes called the love hormone as it gives you
a sense of calm and well-being. The perfect remedy!

OK, that's enough crying now, stop it.

Recommended for: The emotional roller-coaster hangover
Not recommended for: The lucky escape hangover

Sleep

If you can sleep through a hangover, it's the best thing you can do. Throughout the preceding night, alcohol will have affected your sleep patterns and stopped you from entering a good, restorative deep sleep. Hence when you wake up, even if you've managed to sleep till noon, you will feel tired. You've been in a state of unconsciousness rather than soundly asleep.

Your body will be craving some decent shut-eye. If you can get some now, then do. Which is not always possible, of course, as you may need to be awake to attend to a child, go to work or even worse be violently sick down a toilet. In which case, you're now on an endurance mission until you can finally get some sleep.

Good bloomin' morning

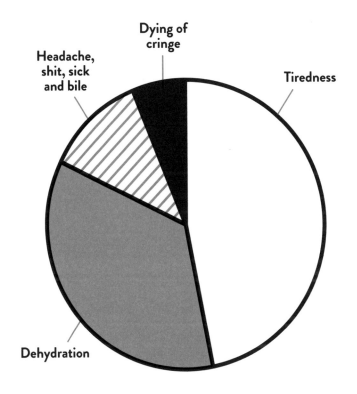

The major hangover symptoms

Recommended for: All hangovers

IV drips and oxygen bars

These are the sort of thing they have in that there London. Hipster hangover cures that are almost certainly placebo over substance.

IV drip

The IV drip cure is a bag of saline solution containing vital nutrients (including water, of course) placed straight into your bloodstream via a needle. The IV cure has been recently been made popular by knobheads with too much money and TikTok accounts to promote. The premise of avoiding your current abomination of a digestive system is a good one, but at a cost of around £150 per hour for a session, you would do well to stop pretending you're a billionaire playboy and have a pint of water with an effervescent vitamin C tablet in it like the rest of us.

Oxygen bars

Oxygen bars are a craze sweeping gullible people all over the world. Pay through the nose for a 20-minute treatment of fresh air enriched with 40 per cent oxygen. The supposed benefits are that you will be supplying your body with extra oxygen and helping to reinvigorate your bloodstream.

If you're healthy and well, your oxygen saturation in your bloodstream will be at round 99 per cent anyway. An oxygen mask will do nothing for this saturation level. It's like trying to top up a completely full glass of water, with more water. Idiotic.

Recommended for: People with more money than sense
Not recommended for: Most hangovers

Feeling like a prize plum hanging out at the oxygen bar

"WINE IS SUNLIGHT HELD TOGETHER BY WATER"

Galileo Galilei

"WILL YOU CLOSE THAT BLOODY CURTAIN MY HEAD IS POUNDING"

Galileo Galilei after
too much 'sunlight'

Recovery 'recipes'

Recovery 'recipes'

Everyone who has had a hangover also has a crazy hangover
cure that has worked for them. Hangover cures can be
personal things, not to be joked about.

The late, great, chef Anthony Bourdain was no stranger
to a hangover cure and was once asked for his best
recommendation: 'Take aspirin, drink cold cola, smoke a joint,
eat some spicy Szechuan food ... works every time.'
Well, let's see Anthony, let's see.

Scrambled eggs

Scrambled eggs on toast are a classic hangover cure. Low in fat, high in protein and there's a good hit of carbs from the toast. Eggs contain a high amount of cysteine, a chemical that helps you clear out alcohol from your system.

If you're feeling fancy, vegan or just want to appear smug, scrambled tofu also contains cysteine and tastes great on toast. Grab some silken tofu, add in black salt and turmeric and serve on sourdough with a chai latte. Simply delicious, sweetie.

A banana

A banana is packed with potassium, sugar and fibre. All great elements of a hangover cure. Bananas are soft and comforting, easy to eat and feel good for you. If you want to feel like you're doing something healthy after the night before, a banana is the thing.

Level up a banana by mushing it up and spreading it on white sliced bread to eat as a banana butty. This will add in some of those quick-access, filthy carbs your body is craving.

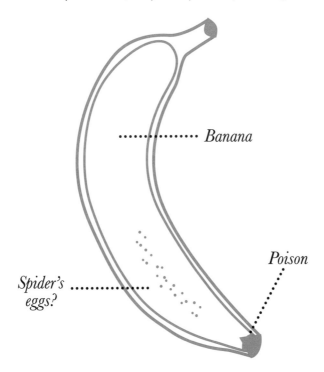

Banana

Poison

Spider's eggs?

Chicken noodle soup

A warm, comforting broth, high in sodium and hydration. Stick some noodles in and you have the recipe for a good hangover survival meal.

Don't have the time to create a clear consommé? Make a decent stock using a stock cube and whatever vegetables you can muster from the salad drawer of the fridge (carrot, leek, celery and an onion are all ideal). Add in some fresh noodles and lemon, ginger and garlic to taste. Heat through and serve.

Vegetables

Lemon

Garlic and ginger

Chicken stock

Ordering a pizza

One of the best cures for a hangover is stuffing carbs – many, many carbs – down your throat. Carbs are the food that give you energy and make your body work. So the ideal food for you right now. And the easiest way to get a shit-ton of those carbs? Ordering a pizza. The complex recipe is as follows: order a pizza.

If you are short on cash then five rounds of hot buttered toast will have the same effect on your body, but at a fraction of the cost and the calorie count.

Getting all lofty whilst on the phone to Sammy's Pizza

Bacon sandwich

A hangover calls for all of the comfort foods. Foods like bread, pasta, noodles and oats are all high on the list of a hangover sufferer's cravings list. Your body's blood sugar level has dipped and the carbs found in these foods, especially the filthy versions of them (no wholewheat here), will get them spiking no end. Comfort food does what it says; it comforts and soothes you.

Balance out the carbs with a hit of salty protein and add in a little sugary kick from the ketchup (which also contains vitamin C) and you have yourself a perfect hangover breakfast. A bacon sandwich!

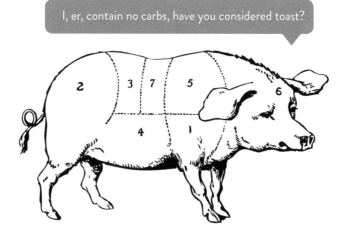

A fry-up

If you ask any medical professional if a fry-up cures a hangover they will resoundingly say, 'No, of course not. Eat fresh fruit and porridge instead, and how did you get into my house?' Contrary to this sound advice, a fry-up is regularly touted as an ideal hangover cure by morons who claim that 'grease soaks up the alcohol'.

These morons are painfully ignorant of how a digestive tract works and will also claim that sick is stored in the back of your legs and that pee is stored in the balls.

A hangover drastically affects your body's digestive system, making it harder to digest food such as meat, dairy products and fatty foods, the key ingredients in a standard fry-up. Hitting your body with a 'Belly Buster' special from the local greasy spoon cafe is going to prove taxing and might even end up with you making a 'call on the big white telephone', i.e. being horrifically sick. Stick to the mug of tea and a few rounds of toast.

'But didn't you suggest a bacon sandwich on the previous page?' I hear you whimper. The difference with a bacon sandwich is that the balance of fat, carbohydrates and protein is far better. It's not a plate swimming in grease, but a hit of all three macro nutrients in one.

If you are insistent on eating a fry-up as a cure for a hangover don't skimp on the beans, tomatoes and mushrooms and for god's sake leave the fried bread out.

A crisp sandwich

A crisp sandwich (or butty) is a simple pleasure for painful times. When actual cooking is definitely off the agenda for your poor fragile little body.

To prepare a crisp sandwich, start by taking some cheap white sliced bread, put that sourdough back in the bread bin, no complex poncey flavours needed here. Butter the bread to add some necessary moisture and load up with your crisp of choice.

You can of course go potato-crisp-based, e.g. a classic salt and vinegar or prawn cocktail, but to really get the most out of a crisp sandwich you want to investigate the world of the puffed corn snack. We are talking Wotsits, Quavers, Space Raiders and Quarterbacks (do they still make those?).

Possibly consider a sauce? Don't go rogue with your sauce choices, though – just stick to red, brown or white (mayo), depending on how posh you feel.

Go for a triple layer for maximum recovery from a hangover. Think of a triple-layer crisp sandwich like a poor man's lasagne. Layer of carbs, layer of flavour, layer of carbs etc. Why not mix up the flavour on each layer?
Hey, look at you go, you're Heston Blumenthal!

Cheese toastie

In many ways, the cheese toastie is the 'hot crisp sandwich'
of the hungover culinary world. Beautifully simple but
ultimately extremely satisfying.

To make the perfect cheese toastie, find the toastie maker that's
been languishing in the junk cupboard in the kitchen for years. The
noise of the clattering Tupperware alone will wake you up. Give it a
dust and identify if the bits stuck to it are just old cheese crusts or
in fact mouse droppings or dead insects. It's probably fine,
so plug it in and listen to it fizz into life.

Butter some bread, grate some cheese and construct your toastie.

Take a moment to consider where this toastie maker actually came
from. The origin of a decent old toastie maker is rarely known, lost
in the mists of time along with who bought you that Pyrex
dish and where the sodding lid for it has gone.

When your toastie is cooked, do remember that the insides are
molten cheese and will burn the roof of your mouth so badly you
won't be able to taste for a week, so leave it a minute to cool. Use
this time to add a splodge of dipping sauce for the crusts.

Avocado toast

Although avocado toast is a very healthy breakfast, ideal for a hangover, the true power of avocado toast to cure a hangover is found in smugness alone. Mash avocado in a bowl with a twist of lemon, salt, pepper and chilli flakes and spread onto toast. It will make you feel like you're a health queen who actually cares for their body. Wilfully ignoring the very real evidence to the contrary given your current stinking hangover.

Feeling extra smug? Spread your avocado onto artisan sourdough and call it 'avo toast'. Before long you will find yourself in your East London flat, nursing a craft IPA hangover, saying, 'Yah, Sebastian, we totes have to yonk the recipe for this tahini drizz that Izzy wazzed on our bodacious avo' toast this arvo, bangin maaaaaaaate.'
Or whatever it is you young people say these days.

A roast

A roast dinner, like a cup of tea, is the British cure for everything. Feeling down? Have a roast. Feeling hungover? Roast.

There are many variations centred around meat, but the real key ingredient is roast potatoes, smothered in gravy. Choose your trimmings specific to your meat choice (stuffing for chicken, crackling for pork). But a Yorkshire pudding is a must for all roast dinners.

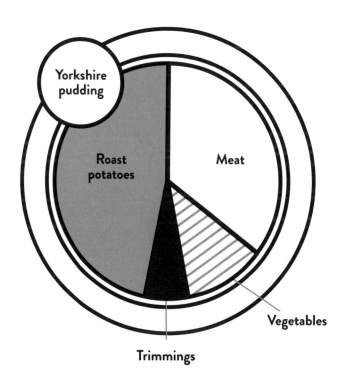

Mac & cheese

If you have the foresight to prepare a mac & cheese the day before a drinking session then this recipe is for you. For the love of god do not attempt to make a mac & cheese with a hangover. It will end in tears, a small fire and lasting damage to the infrastructure of the entire street.

Mac & cheese consists of mac (macaroni) and cheese (cheese) and is the ultimate comfort food, just right for a hangover. A large cheesy hug from the food that never judges you for your pissed-up indiscretions.

To make a mac & cheese, boil up some macaroni and set to one side, whilst you make a cheese sauce. There are a few versions of this depending on how fancy you feel:

Low effort
Grate some cheese onto your hot macaroni and stir until melted. It's technically a mac & cheese, sue me.

Medium effort
Start a roux by melting some butter in a saucepan, add in a couple of spoons of flour and stir until you make a paste. Whisk in milk little by little over the heat to create a thick sauce. Dump a shit-load of grated cheese in the sauce. Hey presto, cheese sauce!

Maximum, smug vegan effort
Replace the butter and milk for non-dairy options. Add some blended cashew nuts to the sauce along with a decent amount of Nooch (nutritional yeast). Stir and eat with a lofty, judgy attitude.

Attempting a hungover mac & cheese

Haejangguk

Haejangguk translates roughly as hangover soup and is served in Korea where it is consumed by weary drinkers. It's rich in vitamins, minerals and wholesome goodness – everything you want from a hangover cure.

To make your hangover soup, simply stick everything in a big pot and bring to the boil, then allow to simmer for a few minutes to soften the cabbage and bring out the flavour of the stock. If you can't stomach the chilli just leave that out of the recipe. If you don't like cabbage then probably look for a different hangover survival food.

1 blanched napa cabbage

1 tbsp doenjang, 1 tbsp gochujang

4 garlic cloves

2 tbsp soy sauce

1 chilli and spring onion

5 cups of beef stock

Pancakes

Pancakes are good for a hangover; it's to do with the tossing. A good toss will stave off most hangovers for a few hours.

If you don't have the strength for a toss, American-style pancakes are ideal. Mix together 200g self-raising flour, 200ml milk, 1.5 tsp baking powder and three big eggs into a batter and pour into a hot frying pan. Flip halfway through cooking and serve hot with maple syrup and fresh fruit.

I've tossed off three times this morning!

A champion tosser at work

Cola

A little known 'fact' you can find on Google (along with evidence that the moon landings were faked) is that cola was invented as a hangover cure. What a revelation!

So going by Google, in 1734 Dr Charles Fanta, suffering with a raging hangover, sat down and concocted a recipe for a tonic so powerful that it would banish any hangover. It being the past his tonic was loaded with ridiculous ingredients ranging from the unusual to the downright illegal – yes, cocaine was once in Coke. Which might sort your hangover out but then you're opening a whole Pandora's box of other problems.

An ice-cold cola is full of hydration from water, quick-access energy from sugar and the livener of a shot of caffeine. Don't be fooled into a 'zero' or 'diet' version as it has none of the bad stuff that will make you feel great right now.

The other element of this hangover cure is the temperature of the beverage. Ice-cold is the only acceptable temperature; any warmer and you might as well be drinking piss. An easy way to prepare for your hangover is by putting in your cola into the fridge the night before. If you really want to go that extra mile you can store a glass in the freezer overnight to pour out into. Don't be alarmed if your hands or tongue get stuck to the glass though, they should loosen eventually.

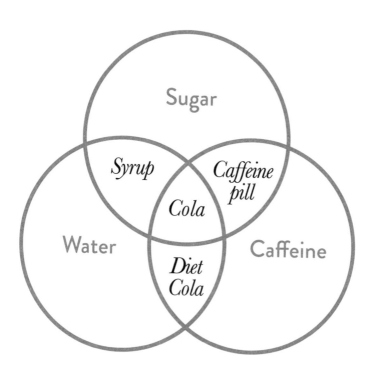

Isotonic sports drinks

Still isotonic sports drinks are supposedly designed to help rebalance your electrolytes and hydration after a sports session. They are rich in sodium, potassium, magnesium, and calcium and have the magic word 'isotonic' on them because 'science'.

What sports drinks are predominantly used for all over the world, however, is curing a hangover. So much science, just to stop you feeling like shit.

Sports drinks also contain a decent amount of energy, in the form of carbohydrates, and fluids to help you rehydrate.

OK that's isotonic squash sorted: next, curing cancer

Scientists making 'important' discoveries

Pickle juice

Pickle juice

Yes you heard. Pickle juice. The juice from a jar of pickles.
People drink that to cure hangovers. I know, madness.

Pickle juice does actually contain high amounts of sodium and
potassium, two electrolytes that will be lost after a night of drinking.
So pickle juice might actually restore your electrolytes and help with
hydration. Just don't drink too much, as the acetic acid in the pickle
juice (the vinegar) may cause stomach upsets and give you a case of
the shits. As if you need that added to your symptoms right now.

People please, Lucozade is a thing.

Tea

If you're British you will know that a cup of tea will cure all ills. So it stands to reason that tea will cure a hangover. A cup of tea contains three of the key ingredients of a hangover cure: hydration, caffeine and antioxidants.

The water in the tea will hydrate your body, the caffeine will provide you with stimulation and energy to get out of bed and the antioxidants somehow help mop up the alcohol, but as you will appreciate I am not a scientist and this is not science. Go with it.

Is tea better than coffee for a hangover? Well, it contains less caffeine which is a downside but this also means that it's more hydrating which is an upside. You can certainly drink a decent vat of tea without adding shakes and caffeine convulsions to your list of symptoms.

The most powerful medicine on earth

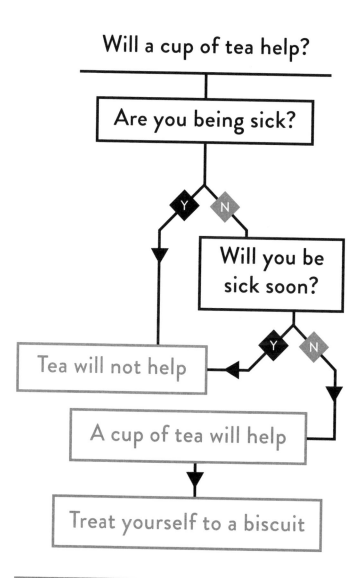

Will a cup of tea help?

Are you being sick?

Will you be sick soon?

Tea will not help

A cup of tea will help

Treat yourself to a biscuit

Coffee

Some people can't seemingly exist without coffee in the morning on a normal day (if 'hilarious' posts on Facebook are to be believed). So it follows naturally that coffee for a hangover is a great idea. A shot of caffeine will prime your system to deal with your tired body and slovenly brain. Make it a double shot and surely you will soon be on the straight and narrow.

For the best hangover coffee cure, make sure to drink strong black coffee. No milk, cream or other additives needed.

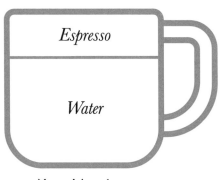

Normal Americano

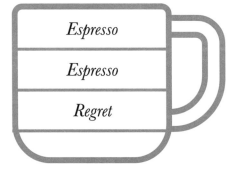

Hangover Americano

Hair of the dog

'Hair of the dog' is short for 'hair of the dog that bit you', which to be honest makes even less sense. The basic theory is that when you're drunk you can't feel any hangover effects. Acquire some more booze and drink it, thus getting you drunk again. Now this is a problem for 'future you' to deal with. But know this: 'future you' thinks 'now you' is an arsehole.

If you want to be high and mighty about it and feel less like an alcoholic you can quote Ancient Greek physician Hippocrates, the father of modern medicine, who claimed that '*similia similibus curantur*' or 'like cures like'. For example, say you drank three bottles of red wine and have a hangover. Simply drink another glass of red wine and 'hey presto', the hangover has disappeared. There are two main problems with this theory. The first is stomaching another glass of red wine in the morning is quite a tricky ordeal and secondly this theory is also the basis for homeopathy which is of course a giant crock of shit.

If you are sold on the hair-of-the-dog approach then you must do it correctly. There is a family of morning-after cocktails called 'the corpse revivers'. These are viciously strong and potent – said to be strong enough to wake the dead. In truth they are vile and you'll be lucky not to see these again all down the front of your already filthy pyjamas. Go have a shower.

The corpse reviver

Variation, with absinthe ... wtf?

Come on, that's ridiculous

This is just madness

Bloody mary

A hangover cure classic and for very good reason. A bloody mary is a large glass of tomato juice, spiced with hot sauce and Worcestershire sauce, seasoned with salt and pepper and pepped up with a shot of vodka. Often served with a stick of celery and wedge of lemon. Bloody marys can vary widely from place to place in terms of how they are seasoned and served. The two key parts are vodka and tomato juice but they must never be served with just these two ingredients alone.

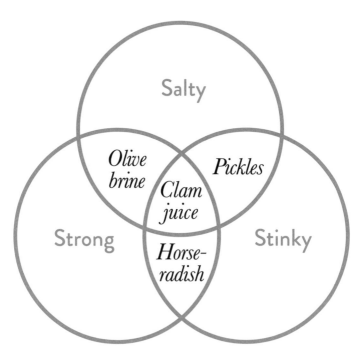

Additional ingredients for a bloody mary

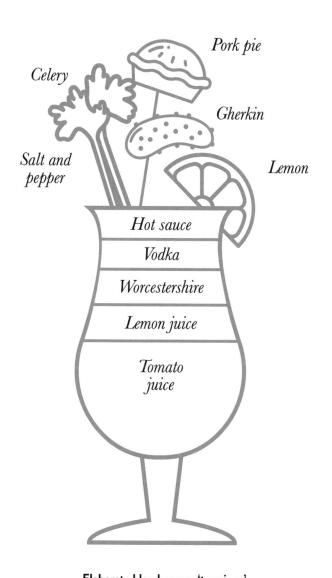

Pork pie

Celery

Gherkin

Salt and
pepper

Lemon

Hot sauce

Vodka

Worcestershire

Lemon juice

Tomato
juice

Elaborate bloody mary 'toppings'

Hangman's blood

The strongest hangover remedy around. It's illegal to serve in a bar in the UK as it contains a ludicrous amount of alcohol. If you're hungover this will cure it but it will give you a far worse problem in that you are almost instantly absolutely pissed again, well done.

Seriously, don't make this cocktail, it's a bad idea. If you do have the ingredients in the house and you're considering making this, please see the final chapter.

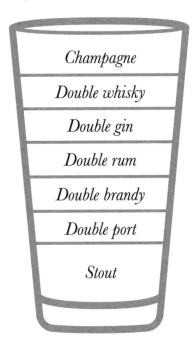

Champagne

Double whisky

Double gin

Double rum

Double brandy

Double port

Stout

This is why we can't have nice things

Prairie oyster

The prairie oyster is probably what Jeeves served Wooster in
P. G. Wodehouse's 1916 short story 'Jeeves Takes Charge'.
It's not explicitly named but the ingredients are all there.

Some hangover cures seem to exist purely as a disgusting punishment
to purge all your wrongdoing from last night. The prairie oyster is
one such cure. It consists of a raw egg yolk in a glass with a dash of
Worcestershire sauce and hot sauce. Seasoned with salt and pepper
and downed whole. Then, presumably, the consumer struggles to
avoid retching themselves into next week. The consistency is that of
a raw oyster but without any of the charm or flavour of the oyster.
So it's just the bogey-like texture, nice!

As a variation you may add tomato juice in small quantities so as to
be reminiscent of a bloody mary (or virgin mary in this case). This
variation is a tiny bit more palatable at the very least.

"YOU CAN'T GET A HANG- OVER...

IF YOU DON'T STOP DRINKING"

A bona fide moron

Avoiding hangovers

Avoiding hangovers

The best way to limit the severity of a hangover is to deal with it at the source, i.e. the night before. Prevention is better than cure, after all. There are many old wives' tales around that supposedly help with avoiding a hangover; most are obviously bullshit and some are just common sense. There is also a thriving industry in supplements and pills that you can take before a night out containing all manner of snake oil. The best way to avoid a hangover? Don't drink at all. But you don't want to hear that, do you? Fine, read on, here are some ways that *might* reduce a hangover.

Eat before you go out

Eating food before you start drinking is an excellent way to get less drunk. It will affect the way you feel during and after a heavy drinking session. Having food in your stomach will keep you feeling full, keep your blood sugar levels up and will slow down the emptying of your stomach which in turn slows down the rate at which alcohol enters your bloodstream. Purely from a physical angle, your stomach will be mostly full so there will be less space to fit drink in. It's a win-win. There are good things and bad things to eat before a heavy 'sesh' of course.

Pickled eggs
High in protein and a good weighty food, guaranteed to clog you up for hours. Just don't eat 20 pickled eggs for a dare before going out for a drink, as it will completely ruin the night. Yes, this is oddly specific for a very good reason.

Oats
Filling and full of fibre, oats will help keep you full but also nice and 'regular' in the morning. Oats also help your liver function and so are a perfect defence against alcohol.

Brightly coloured soup
This will have no benefit at all but will look excellent when you puke it up onto the pavement outside the Wetherspoons.

Don't mix your drinks

Mixing your drinks won't get you drunker (that's a bit of an old wives' tale), but you might become more confused about how much you've drunk over the evening. Especially if you're swapping between wine, beer and shots.

Another thing to consider is that if you were to put all the random drinks you're chugging into a mixing bowl and give it a good old stir, it would probably produce a mad curdled mess. Certainly not a mix that would be conducive to a settled stomach. It's wise to stick to the same sort of drinks all night.

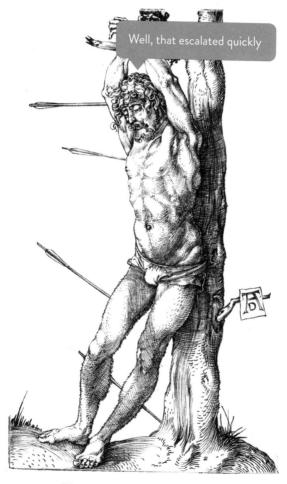

Blaming it all on the last bottle of
house red and yard of ale chaser

Drink clear drinks

When alcohol is made in drinks, a cheeky little by-product of the process that find its way into the drink is a select group of compounds called congeners.

It's not important to know what they are, but it's important to know what they do. They are not really things you want too many of in your blood as they cause all manner of problems. They also hang around your bloodstream, like a fart in a sleeping bag, waiting to be mopped up along with the alcohol. They slow your body's recovery process down to a snail's pace.

Wilfully mishearing 'let's avoid congeners' for 'let's all do the conga!'

The more distilled a drink is the fewer congeners it has, so a good rule of thumb is that the clearer the drink, the fewer congeners will be in there:

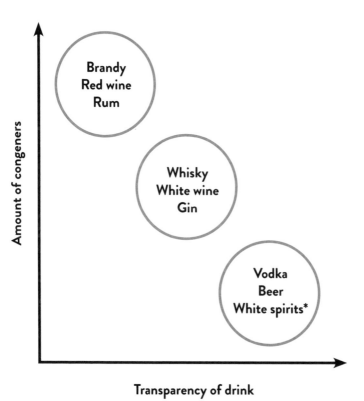

*Don't drink white spirits, that's clearly a joke.

Go to bed!

Lack of a good night's sleep is one of the main reasons a hangover feels so bad, so it stands to reason that if you go to bed in a good amount of time you should help your hangover no end. The problem being that even if you have made it to bed the alcohol in your body will disrupt your natural sleep pattern. Meaning you don't get enough of that lovely, delicious deep sleep, the sleep that your body uses to repair and replenish itself.

Going to bed earlier might not make you sleep better but what it does do is get you out of the way of all the fuckery. It you're in bed you can't be up and about fucking around. The late hours of a drinking session are where the really bad decisions are made, the final drinks are glugged and the kitchen is raided for drinking sherry and that tiny bit of advocaat left over from Christmas 2009.

At least I'm in bed, I'll deal with the tentacles in the morning

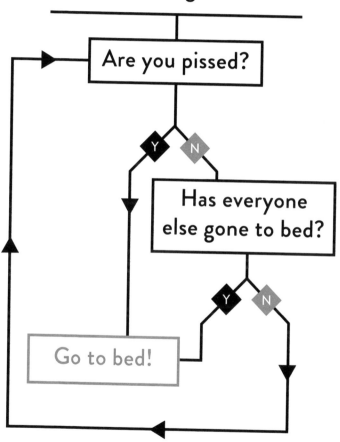

Is it time to go to bed?

Are you pissed?

Y   N

Has everyone else gone to bed?

Y   N

Go to bed!

Drink water every other drink

This method of drinking water throughout a night out is widely touted around as a great way to avoid a hangover. The system is clear: every drink of alcohol you have you should in turn drink a glass of water.

The theory is that as you are drinking water you are pre-loading the water for the morning, combating the dehydration before it happens. Also you are consuming less alcohol because you've got to drink a sodding glass of water every other drink.

The theory is fine, but in reality, what actually happens is that you start the method with all good intentions and then get pissed and forget. Or you are constantly trotting off to the toilet to take a leak because of the gallons of water you're drinking, making it look like you are actually going there for another reason involving class-A drugs.

Then you realise you're four or five drinks away from your last glass of water but you don't have the strength of character to go and ask the barman for four glasses of water and you quickly give up. System. Ruined.

A really smart thing to do, and one that is much more manageable if you are not completely smashed, is to drink a large pint of water right before going to bed and keep another glass by the bedside for when you wake up. You can then tell everyone about this hack like you invented it. Why not? Everyone else does.

You, reading this chapter knowing full well you
won't do a single thing from it

"NEVER AGAIN"

You

"LET'S DO SHOTS"

Also you

Drinking in moderation

Drinking in moderation

It's not exactly rocket science, is it? Drink less and your hangover will be reduced. If you are lucky enough to be one of those people you read about who can drink a just a glass of wine with dinner and then nothing else, or have a pint at lunch that doesn't end up at 3am in a curry house falling asleep into your madras then drinking in moderation might just be the thing for you. If you have been trying to moderate all along and you're accustomed to the aforementioned 3am curry house trip then see the final chapter.

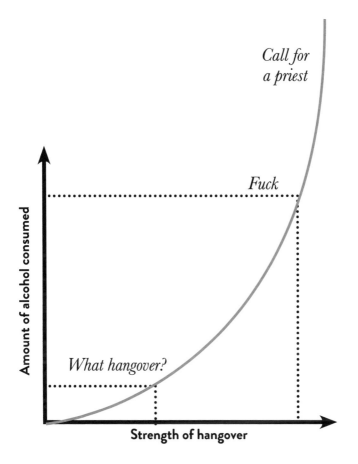

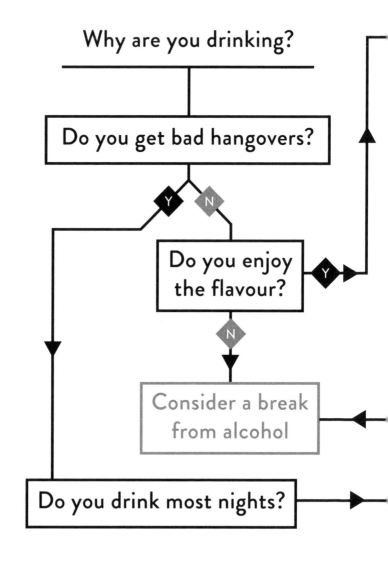

Why are you drinking?

Do you get bad hangovers?

Y   N

Do you enjoy the flavour?

Y

N

Consider a break from alcohol

Do you drink most nights?

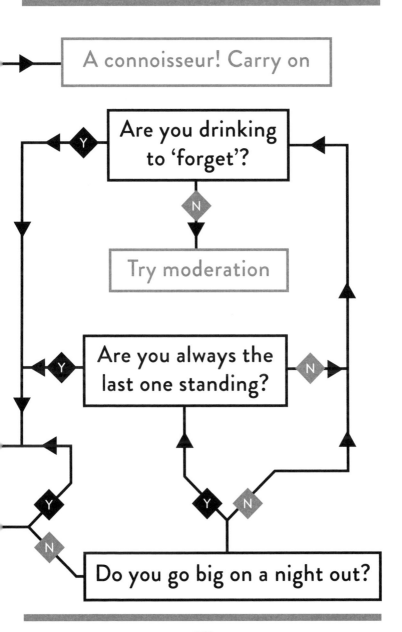

Cutting down

If quantity of drink is a problem for you, why not try drinking lower-strength drinks, go for a single rather than a double or try a lighter beer, and for god's sake don't do shots.

If you are able to moderate the amount you drink and how often you drink then you're already on the right track to reducing the severity and number of hangovers you experience.

If you struggle to moderate because of social pressures, as it's no longer the 1970s you can communicate to the people you're out with that you are trying to drink less. If they give you shit about it then they are shitty toxic friends. But that's a subject for a different book: *How to Deal with Shitty Friends*.

'Tis but a tiny triple vodka

How to moderate your drinks

Do you want another?

Y — N

Don't have another drink

Are you tipsy?

N — Y

Do you have work in the morning?

Y

N

Keep track of what you drink

If you want to cut down on what you're drinking, it's important to know what you're actually drinking in the first place. To do that we will need to keep track of what you are drinking over the course of a week or two. Be brutally honest or this process will be a completely pointless exercise.

You can use one of many apps on your phone to track your drinks or you can go old-school and use a little notepad. Note down what you drink and what measure it is (pint of beer, half a shandy, yard of lager). When making drinks at home use a measure, don't just guess what a shot is – you don't work at a top cocktail bar'*, you can't free-pour 25ml by eye!

If you are at a friend's house, keep an eye out for them topping up your wine glass as this can make it notoriously difficult to keep track of how much you've had to drink. You can easily end up thinking you've only had one drink but the purple lips and teeth say otherwise.

*You might work at a cocktail bar, in which case well done, continue to pour by eye.

Plan ahead

Decide how much you want to drink and when. Planning ahead and sticking to it is what moderation is all about.

If you find sticking to the plan difficult, work out what triggers you to drink or to have another drink. Maybe it's a certain group of friends or a place where you always end up having a skin-full of drink in.

A plan for the night might involve focusing on the quantity of drink, imposing a three-drink limit, for example. Or it might be to plan how to turn down a drink when you feel like you've had enough (this assumes you will know when you have had enough).

Cutting down if you're drinking at home can be problematic. Easy option is to try to keep little or no alcohol in the house. Hard option is to keep a massive amount of delicious alcohol and a working bar in your front room. Choose the easy option.

If you know you're going to be somewhere with people who urge you to drink, plan how you will say no. Practise a 'no thanks' without any hesitations. If you end up with the arsehole who won't take no for an answer (does consent mean nothing to these pricks?) then accept the drink and find a plant pot to pour it into. If all else fails, pull a sickie, or claim you have Covid. Again.

Going out without drinking

Drinking is ingrained in our culture and can be hard to get away from. It's everywhere. Just to socialise of an evening you have to be around alcohol in the pub or a bar, unless you're doing something mad like an archery club or night hikes.

Non-alcoholic drinks have come a long way in the past few years and are more widely available. You can certainly have a half-decent non-alcoholic beer and not really notice the difference.

The real beauty of being sober on a night out? You can drive home. Also most people won't notice the difference in what you're drinking so you can fly under the radar as a sober spy. There will be the odd person who queries why you're not drinking and asks annoying questions whilst standing way too close to you and shouting in your ear. This situation calls for an actual serious chat about drink and now is not the time or the place. Fob them off with an answer like 'I'm just doing it for likes on Instagram'. Awkward social interaction over. You can always follow up with them in the morning with an extremely smug text like 'How's the head, I'm just off for a run'.

If you're out and sober around drunk people, just wait for someone to start repeating themselves and that is your cue to leave. You don't even have to say goodbye, they won't remember if you did. You can just walk out. Bliss.

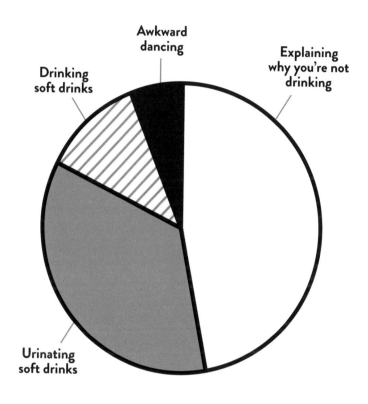

'Sober at a party' activities

Mocktails

Mostly, mocktails are overpriced, over-styled glasses of fruit juice. They are a way to fleece the designated driver, tricking them into thinking that paying £9 for an orange juice with an umbrella in it is somehow delicious.

That said, if you are in a decent cocktail bar there will of course be some interesting alternatives available. You might be missing that tang of alcohol but drink enough and all that sugar syrup will have you bouncing off the walls in no time!

As most mocktails are based around fruit and fruit juice, if you normally drink wine or beer you will be looking for more of a savoury kick. A virgin mary (a bloody mary with the vodka removed) can be delicious but there are only so many cold tomato soups you can drink before you vomit a pink rainbow.

If you're not into getting fleeced for non-alcolhic drinks then choose a strong flavoured mixer on its own, like a tonic or a ginger beer. For god's sake don't fall for the non-alcoholic gin fraud, it really is just heavily flavoured water. A simple tonic water with ice and a slice will see you right and still looks like a nice drink, thus avoiding awkward questions.

A no-hito   A virgin colada

Having a month off

Taking a month off booze is a wonderful way to feel what being sober is like, a little holiday for your booze-beaten body. Having a month off will improve your sleep, hydration and mental health, and increase your productivity. Your liver, stomach and skin will also be in a much better place for not having to cope with alcohol for a while.

You're also saving a massive amount of calories and money by taking a month off. If, for example, you normally drink six pints a week (that's the amount everyone tells their doctor they drink rather than the bleak truth), that is around 5,000 calories a month you have saved, or around 25 delicious doughnuts.

Doing a month clear of booze can help you to have longer periods without alcohol in future. Most people who take part in dry January will begin to drink less when they return to drink. If nothing else it's something you can mention on your Tinder profile.

If you manage to complete a month, before you line up the shots on the bar and get the first round of beers in, take a moment to think if you want to continue with sobriety. If you've done a month, amazing, new personal best!

What people ask you	Your response
'Why are you not drinking?'	'I'm just taking a little break. Have you ever stopped drinking for a while?'
'How long are you not drinking for?'	'No idea, just seeing how long I can go for'
'Booooring!'	'Thank you for your support'
'Are you pregnant?'	'Yes, and it's yours'
'Just have a pint, you big Jessie'	'Go fuck yourself'
'I could never do that'	'You have a drinking problem'

Being sober

Being sober

'Yay, the chapter in this book that no one wants to read!'

'I can't possibly exist without a drink inside me', 'My entire personality is formed around the phrase "prosecco o'clock"; what now for me?'. These might be some of the phrases that go through your head when you consider quitting alcohol.

There is good news and bad; the good news is that being sober is really good for you mentally, physically and for your relationships. The bad news is that being sober is sometimes hard to do.

**The giant elephant in the room that is
your highly apparent drinking problem**

Quitting for good

There might be a day soon where you wake up feeling you've gone too far for the last time and you decide to quit for real. Not just the usual 'I'm never drinking again' nonsense, this time you think you might just mean it.

The thought of never drinking again might be terrifying and feel impossible. How will you have fun? How will you socialise? Aren't sober people all boring bastards?

Make a pros and cons list for continuing to drink and you will quickly realise your life will be so much better without alcohol. There is nothing of any real value on the list of pros for drinking that would in any way encourage you to continue – come on, you can't write 'banter' as a pro, can you? The list of positive things that happen to you and your body when you stop drinking is as long as it is smug. You will improve your physical health, mental health, bank balance, relationships. Your overall smugness will skyrocket. Embrace the smug.

Give it a try, take each day as it comes, don't think too far ahead. You can go a day without drinking, right? Well just do that over and over until it becomes a habit.

Do you need actual help?

If you need support from someone, ask for it. There might be someone you love or a friend who understands, reach out to them and tell them you are struggling. Alcoholics Anonymous, a group who are often the butt of a joke for heavy drinkers, is the ideal place to go. It's a safe space to go and talk to people who understand exactly what it's like to feel the nagging addiction of alcohol. Don't do this alone.

For many of us, childhood is the happiest, most carefree time of our lives, and you know what's missing from childhood? Alcohol. Find the child in you that knew how to have fun without a cheeky vimto and being sick on someone's shoes.

Get sober mates

The easiest way to fail at being sober is to have toxic friends around you who can't seem to cope with you not drinking. Your sobriety is casting a light onto their own drinking habits. They tend to get a little defensive and offer unsolicited excuses for their own drinking. It's tiresome.

If you have friends like these, you need to find some sober mates. If you don't have any sober friends at all then look around for a new hobby or group to join.

When you do find them, meet up with sober friends to talk through stupid things pissed people have said to you, embarrassing things you did whilst drinking, and ways you're coping now. It really helps.

What drunk people say	What they mean
'You're no fun now'	'I don't know how to have fun without alcohol'
'Just have one, I won't tell anyone'	'I don't understand boundaries'
'I don't have a drinking problem'	'I do have a drinking problem'
'Frzxz bllrub nn the juzz'	'I should go to bed'

Get into fitness

You've proved you have an addictive personality by having to stop drinking, so why not throw that addictive trait of yours into a healthy pursuit like fitness or something mad like CrossFit. It's a massive cliché of course – reformed drinker gets into fitness – but there is a reason people do it. Fitness activities are ones that happen during the day and not around alcohol. They give you the endorphin hit you're missing from getting smashed, but they also have the opposite effect of alcohol on your body. You're actually making it better!

It's a great way to chase your old drinking buddies away as they will be so bored of you telling them about your insane workouts. Anyway, you won't need them soon as you'll have lots of new gym friends, and they have abs. So you decide who is better?

"DRINK BECAUSE YOU'RE HAPPY...

...BUT NEVER BECAUSE YOU'RE MISERABLE"

G. K. Chesterton

About the author

My first day of sobriety was 22 May 2017. I am currently six years sober. I'm proof that you can be sober and still act like a complete and utter knob. I know my actions are my choice rather than the drink controlling me. Being sober is freedom.

After turning sober I broke two Guinness World Records for the sack race. Something I wouldn't have been able to do with a hangover or carrying that literal beer belly. If you have the merest thought about giving up drink, I urge you to give it a go, try a month off to start. It's the best decision I ever made.

I haven't had a hangover in six years and
I am painfully smug about it.

Then

Now

People I know that are probably alcoholics

Jason Kimington, Luke Enfield, Rachel Stoppard,
Jim Lightning, Simon Yately, Clive Sinclair (no, not that one),
Tracy Polymath, Ronald Macintosh, Sir George Featherington
Carstairs, Becky Bollocks, Susan Fingers, Matthew Mornington
Crescent, Duke Diagram, Ronnie Pickles, Jay Barratt, Chris
Chang, Laura McPartlin, Colin Messy, Donna Winter, Sam
Frencho, Alan Anderton, Bill Carr, Mike Oxlong, Isabelle
Ringing, Eileen Sideways.

Obviously these are not real names,
but if you checked the list looking for yours
then, surprise! You have a drinking problem.

1

Pop Press, an imprint of Ebury Publishing
20 Vauxhall Bridge Road
London SW1V 2SA

Pop Press is part of the Penguin Random House group of companies whose
addresses can be found at global.penguinrandomhouse.com

First published by Pop Press in 2023

www.penguin.co.uk

A CIP catalogue record for this book is available from the British Library

ISBN: 9781529913675

Printed and bound by TBB, as. Slovakia

The authorised representative in the EEA is Penguin Random House Ireland,
Morrison Chambers, 32 Nassau Street, Dublin D02 YH68